T008891?

THE FOURTH MASQUERADE

POEMS

Kraftgriots

Also in the series (POETRY)

David Cook *et al*: *Rising Voices*
Olu Oguibe: *A Gathering Fear;* winner, 1992 All Africa Okigbo prize for Literature
    & Honourable mention, 1993 Noma Award for Publishing in Africa
Nnimmo Bassey: *Patriots and Cockroaches*
Okinba Launko: *Dream-Seeker on Divining Chain*
Onookome Okome: *Pendants,* winner, 1993 ANA/Cadbury poetry prize
Nnimmo Bassey: *Poems on the Run*
Ebereonwu: *Suddenly God was Naked*
Tunde Olusunle: *Fingermarks*
Joe Ushie: *Lambs at the Shrine*
Chinyere Okafor: *From Earth's Bedchamber*
Ezenwa-Ohaeto: *The Voice of the Night Masquerade,* joint-winner, 1997 ANA/
    Cadbury poetry prize
George Ehusani: *Fragments of Truth*
Remi Raji: *A Harvest of Laughters,* joint-winner 1997 ANA/Cadbury poetry prize
Patrick Ebewo: *Self-Portrait & Other Poems*
George Ehusani: *Petals of Truth*
Nnimmo Bassey: *Intercepted*
Joe Ushie: *Eclipse in Rwanda*
Femi Oyebode: *Selected Poems*
Ogaga Ifowodo: *Homeland & Other Poems,* winner, 1993 ANA poetry prize
Godwin Uyi Ojo: *Forlorn Dreams*
Tanure Ojaide: *Delta Blues and Home Songs*
Niyi Osundare: *The Word is an Egg* (2000)
Tayo Olafioye: *A Carnival of Looters* (2000)
Ibiwari Ikiriko: *Oily Tears of the Delta* (2000)
Arnold Udoka: *I am the Woman* (2000)
Akinloye Ojo: *In Flight* (2000)
Joe Ushie: *Hill Songs* (2000)
Ebereonwu: *The Insomniac Dragon* (2000)
Deola Fadipe: *I Make Pondripples* (2000)
Remi Raji: *Webs of Remembrance* (2001)
'Tope Omoniyi: *Farting Presidents and Other Poems* (2001)
Tunde Olusunle: *Rhythm of the Mortar* (2001)
Abdullahi Ismaila: *Ellipsis* (2001)
Tayo Olafioye: *The Parliament of Idiots: Tryst of the* Sinators (2002)
Femi Abodunrin: *It Would Take Time: Conversation with Living Ancestors* (2002)
Nnimmo Bassey: *We Thought It Was Oil But It Was Blood* (2002)
Ebi Yeibo: *A Song For Tomorrow and Other Poems* (2003)
Adebayo Lamikanra: *Heart Sounds* (2003)
Ezenwa-Ohaeto: *The Chants of a Minstrel* (2003), winner, 2004 ANA/NDDC poetry
    prize and joint-winner, 2005 LNG The Nigeria Prize for Literature
Seyi Adigun: *Kalakini: Songs of Many Colours* (2004)

THE FOURTH MASQUERADE
POEMS

Ebi Yeibo

kraftgriots

Published by
Kraft Books Limited
6A Polytechnic Road, Sango, Ibadan
Box 22084, University of Ibadan Post Office
Ibadan, Oyo State, Nigeria
℡ +234803 348 2474, 805 129 1191
E-mail: kraftbooks@yahoo.com
www.kraftbookslimited.com

First published 2014

ISBN 978–978–918–169–8

= KRAFTGRIOTS =
(A literary imprint of Kraft Books Limited)

First printing, June 2014

Dedication

For my parents,
George German Yeibo &
Saijorce Yeibo,
Who forged my being
With the Almighty's seal
And, with passionate strokes,
Painted the rainbow
Across my sky ...

Acknowledgements

Many thanks to E.E. Sule, Ogaga Okuyade, Austine Amanze Akpuda, Sunday Awhefeada, Ben Binebai, Ebinyo Ogbowei, and O.M. Kwokwo, for the illuminating suggestions and comments; and to my sweetheart, Emee, for the continual prompting and prayers. Above all, to God be the glory, for the unfailing gift of song.

Foreword

The Fourth Masquerade, Yeibo's fifth collection of poems, pushes his artistic impulse and utopian vision further, beyond rage, anger and his unpretentious desire for a moral order which should form the basis and nucleus around which every other thing revolves, in order to realize cosmic balance in the human world. This assertion is easily noticeable in his previous collections. *The Fourth Masquerade* is, however, characterized by an expository temper coupled with a cautionary tone one identifies with age and experience. The raging tone of protest is not completely absent from this collection, but it is encapsulated in ethnomoral metaphors geared towards re-ordering the human conscience. As one of the most important Nigerian poets who continue to write the nation in verse, Yeibo has strategically fashioned a kind of poetry that does not only derive its idiom from the prosody and folk tradition of the Izon of Nigeria, it equally advances the poet's vision through form and structure. His recourse to folklore and reliance on oral materials in the image-making process gives coherence and form to the poems. However, what distinguishes this collection from the previous ones is the question of the form through which he demonstrates an intense awareness of the Nigerian experience.

Although Yeibo's poetry has always focused on life in Nigeria and the context of evolving social, cultural, and political events and how geography, economics and politics continue to connive in the contraction of the identity of the Niger Delta people which in turn articulates the devastating condition under which they negotiate their existence in their vanishing habitation, it is the marriage of politics and poetics that makes Yeibo's poetry enduring. Just like no one lives outside of a defined historical moment, Yeibo has never been afraid of or shirked what he fervently believes is his responsibility – the sense of responsibility shaped by his very aesthetic. Yeibo's poetry is inextricably grounded in the post-Shagari social and political transformation down to the millipedic and insoluble phase of the present Nigerian democracy. *The Fourth Masquerade* arguably explores the topography of everyday life in Nigeria. However, the most remarkable aspect of this collection is the eloquent mode with which it reaffirms Yeibo's capacity for articulating concerns other than the apparently political. By this vision, Yeibo has not only expanded the basis for the assessment of his work, but has also demonstrated his poetic ability to engage a variety of poetic conventions and forms. Like I have noted elsewhere, a panoptic appraisal of Yeibo's earlier work, will give expression to the fact that he hardly organizes his poems wholly around a specific thematic orientation. However, in *Shadows of the Setting Sun*, his fourth collection, the poet exhibits an easily discernible ability to organize the poems in the collection around a central idea and the organization of his metaphors and symbols is remarkable. In *The Fourth Masquerade*, Yeibo does not only demonstrate a remarkable competence at exploring several facets of human experience in a poetic idiom grounded in folk tradition – an idiom that does not lend itself to easy signification though, there is a synthesis between form and idiom in the delivery of message. Apparently, therefore, form in *The Fourth Masquerade* does not only give the poems structure, it becomes the textual mechanics or rhetorical design for the re-articulation and reiteration of Yeibo's poetic vision.

The title of the collection is reflective of Yeibo's recourse to a traditional art form indicative of the poetics of orality. Though an ethnocultural metaphor in the poetry of some

Nigerian poets, like the late Ezenwa-Ohaeto[1], it does not only remind one of or evoke a festive ambience and the presence of the supernatural among mere mortals, the masquerade vibrantly establishes the intricate duality and continuity of existence in Africa and the unique union of man, the ancestors and the gods, reminiscent of the occasions of the baptism of Jesus the son of God and the transfiguration where the three spiritual personages that make up the Godhead manifested their distinctiveness before mortals. The masquerade in African metaphysics evokes the possibility of mere mortals transgressing the inelastic limit of their existence. The one who dons the mask carries a special spiritual burden, because at that moment he becomes a confluence of mortals, ancestors and the gods.

Yeibo has continued to express through poetry the relationship between the oppressed Nigerian/African and the rulers. His poetry addresses a deluge of themes and subjects: they include the bureaucratic inefficiency of government, corruption, poverty, infrastructural, moral and institutional decay, the deplorable conditions under which the Niger Delta people negotiate their existence, the vanishing or submerging Niger Deltascape and on some occasions, the lingering effects of colonialism on the African continent. This brings to bear the fact that the struggle for liberation has not in any way ended with the attainment of political independence in Africa. *The Fourth Masquerade* like most contemporary African poetry vibrantly demonstrates the continuous privilege poetry enjoys as the most immediate means of literary expression for the struggle for total liberation since the genre is in its own way an act of acknowledgement of a given reality.

---

[1]   Ezenwa-Ohaeto, *Voice of the Night Masquerade*

The title poem, "The Fourth Masquerade" which is also the first poem sets the tone of the collection. As a poet who continues to sustain a stable relationship with his Izon culture, he becomes attracted to the arts that constantly remind him of his origin and those of common rural folks, the social category he belongs to. Through this attachment to rural life, Yeibo displays his sense of responsibility as a poet by artistically exploiting traditional festivals that are organic to traditional African society[2]. Besides entertainment and the constant reminder about the origins of a people, one other cardinal function of traditional festivals is the ritual of regeneration and transformation of the adherents and their society. The ritual of regeneration and transformation is not whole in itself; rather, it essentialises the importance of reconciliation among humanity and supernatural forces. As I have noted elsewhere, Yeibo's language is gradually becoming elitist. This is easily noticeable in the semantic density of his metaphorical choices. Like the quintessential Yeibo whose linguistic choices are deceptively simple and his subject usually definite and direct, the title poem appears to be evoking a festive mood and an ambience of celebration. This is not far from the point. However, the language and the style of delivery might seem simple and inviting, yet great depth is to be found underneath. These qualities of directness and deceptive simplicity become immediately apparent to anyone who picks this collection for the very first time. As you read on, you discover in no time that you are sailing into the deep waters of puzzlement.

The first poem is not only arresting, it reminds the reader about the fate of mankind and more importantly, the place

---

[2] Dan Izevbaye. "Living the myth: Revisiting Okigbo's art and commitment *Tydskrif Vir Letterkunde,* 48.1, 2011

of the poet metaphorised in the trope of the masquerade. One strategy Yeibo deploys to sustain the tone of the poem is the storytelling motif, which helps him advance meaning. Storytelling is without doubt the most readily accessible and most popular of African traditional oral imaginative forms. Rhetorically, stories are derived from the relationship between man and his environment which make them real. However the teller fantasizes with the real in order to bequeath the tale with universality usually geared towards a moral end. This strategy helps to sustain the idealistic vision of the teller thereby entrenching his own moral impulse, which is usually enduring:

These lines invoke
The frothy salt waters
Of mangrove swamp
In the mild touch of the wind

Sending sensual motions-
Tingling darts of blood-
Through the navel of night
And her dark eyelashes;

These lines are the owl
Hooting ominous messages
In choking pain
In pubescent twilight

The poet locates the people associated with this festival by identifying their physical geography or their physical habitation which is swampy, indicative of the Niger Delta, specifically the Izon of Nigeria: "The frothy salt waters/ Of mangrove swamps". By beginning the collection with a traditional African festival, the poet underscores the centrality of the gods in achieving the poet's vision in this collection. A typical African festival subsumes the spiritual and the physical, represented by masquerades, gods and

11

humanity who must work together. Here the poet and his audience are engaged in a social dialogue geared towards enhancing or creating public accord which one notices in the structural arrangement of the poem. The poem is made of twenty one quatrains, which relate to the kind of symmetry, beauty and harmony that the world would attain if man and the gods work in one accord. Thus the fourth and fifth quatrains do not only carry the tone of caution, they are equally reminders of our nature as humans and what we need to do to attain cosmic balance for a peaceful coexistence in the mortal plane. The rapid association of images in the "burden of being," "blood and dust", "scowling mist" "loaded canoe" and the "raw palm fruit" that "causes cough" are prompters establishing the need for order and conscientious behaviour in human society. A lack of correspondence between man, his environment and supernatural forces produces a clash which in turn introduces elements of disorder and crises.

I think the most humorous and satiric poem in this collection is "For Hamza Al-Mustapha". The poem does not only provoke laughter, it is direct and terse. Yeibo weaves a recent national issue into a popular Ijaw folklore about an elusive fish that is capable of making fun of the fisherman and his fishing paraphernalia no matter how dexterously he deploys his fishing kits. The poem is a paradigm for Nigeria's permeable judicial system. The structural importance of this poem and Yeibo's recourse to orality help advance meaning and embolden his satiric pellet. The poem is a reflection on the impact of corruption, bad governance, the compromised judicial system and their effect upon the moral health of the nation and the socio-economic conditions of the masses. Although the poem centres on the Nigerian judiciary, it profoundly engages the Nigerian ruling class, making it the target of the satiric pill and vitriol.

Though derived from Izon folk tradition, Yeibo invests this poem with such exquisite imagery and emotional intensity that it becomes a thrillingly unique poem. While being satiric, it equally provokes anger especially because of the certainty of freedom the judiciary offers the political class even in the full glare of the masses:

The courts are a torn net
Hauled on the river; roving
Fish have a field day
Swimming through in shiny scorn;

Even the ones caught
Send a telepathic message
To their empathizing kindred
From the home-bound canoe
Through unyielding hyacinth

Not to mourn yet
Until they enter the pot.

Yeibo's poetic reflections on the Niger Delta are not only engaging; they are artistically poignant. Though, he uses politics to invigorate his poetry and sustains the mood with the raging temper of the time, the poems hardly deviate from the sagacity and athleticism of the craft associated with a devoted and seasoned craftsman. A careful appraisal of poems like, "The Wrong Inheritance", "No Festivals Here", "Open Paradox", and "The Delta of Yore" in this collection demonstrates Yeibo's abiding devotion and dedication to the Niger Delta cause and the urgent need to redeem his people and their vanishing homeland from the galloping greed of government and the capitalistic insensitivity of the multinational oil firms. His poems on the Niger Delta do not stand naked as social and environmental rage, Yeibo performs his ethical and social responsibility by linking his natural environment to the bleak and stifling social circumstances of the Niger Delta in particular and the Nigerian nation at large. Interestingly, therefore, Yeibo poignantly harnesses the deltascape to create an atmosphere of gloom and pessimism. His images on the Niger Delta are forceful so that they configure the actual damage brought upon the environment in a cinematographic manner that assaults the human conscience. For example, in "No Festival Here" Yeibo schematically reflects upon the deplorable condition of the environment as a result of oil exploration and exploitation:

Festivals have since recoiled
From streets along the waterway;
Dipped into rabid dungs of memory
Or buried in the overspilling clouds
Taken over the horizon
Scribbling the lean loves
Lining the age, like a kwashiorkor patient.

The festive moments are gone because:

Here a full tide of oil
Breeds milky monsters at the top
Who taunt the treasury
Spitting sore slums and scraps
Though where the water pot stands
There is no dry season;

In "The Wrong Inheritance" Yeibo questions the consistency of the promoters of the amnesty package as a move to massively change the plight of the Niger Delta people and their environment for good though he does not mention the policy:

So something disqualifies
These seekers of peace
On the swirling waves of the creeks

Middlemen who dance on the graves
Of saints sacrificed in the struggle
Who take the lion's share
Of the proceeds of truce
Behind prying eyes

Thus Yeibo's constant resonation of the predicament of the Niger Delta people in his poetry where with a fearless love of truth and keen psychological insight of the despairing ecological drama continuously enacted in the region is not only to specifically signify his patriotism to environmental justice and the Delta cause, he equally draws attention to an institutional failure.

Significantly, the formal structure(one stanza) of the last poem "Mystery" aptly resonates the poet's artistic vision for humanity in this collection: the synergy between man, the ancestors and the gods, as the only pragmatic strategy for human progress. The intervening poems(that is, between the first and last poems) centre on human weaknesses and the continuous fall from the eternal edenic state of being reflected in the formlessness of the poems, an indication of the oppressive social condition where mankind negotiates existence. In contrast, "Mystery" symbolizes a lingering sense of hope for redemption. The poem advocates a union between humans, the ancestors and the gods as a way out of the plight of human existence. Thus, we must understand nature in Yeibo's poems in a double sense because on one level, it exists for its own sake and, on another level, it evokes the poet's social ethos. At a glance, the last poem will confuse the poet's mood as that of nostalgia over the loss of the eternal habitation of the Delta people. However, the poem only draws attention to the answers to humanity's most elusive questions; why are we here? And, how do we survive? The order the poet advocates in the first poem becomes realizable in the last, only if humanity realizes that it is not "a strident taboo":

To look left, where
The shrine was stationed,
So mortals did not
Behold a god's face?

The vision of a possible harmonious society where everything
will be organically whole is only achievable by institutional
checks and balances anchored on time tested moral-ethical
foundation and the commonality of dream between man
and the supernatural world:

O one thought
Man and god needed to tango
In one eternal clasp
Like mortar and pestle
To fashion a decent voyage
Against the roaring tide.

The Fourth Masquerade will always remain remarkable in
the corpus of Yeibo's imaginative composition for two
important reasons. First, it does not merely comment on or
versify social events of everyday life in Nigeria; the poems
also make social, political and historical analysis of these
events and by extension foreground the urgency of a second
independence, negotiable through a synergy between the
gods, ancestors and humanity. Second, one easily notices
the wide range and constancy of Yeibo's vision in this
collection in the way he epigrammatically captures human
flaws through his penetrating power of thought, the artful
deployment of metaphors and the use of folk tradition in
order to defend exalted human values. But more importantly,
most of the poems signal the answers to the eternal questions
confronting humanity.

Ogaga Okuyade, PhD
Niger Delta University, Wilberforce Island,
Bayelsa State, Nigeria.

Contents

A fleet of eagles,
Over the oilbean shadows,
Holds the square
Under curse of their breath.
Christopher Okigbo

Our concessions come
from weakness ....
What have victims not provided
their victors for their own ruin?
The earth is my witness.
Tanure Ojaide

The fourth masquerade

These lines invoke
The frothy salt waters
Of mangrove swamps
In the mild touch of the wind

Sending sensual motions–
Tingling darts of blood–
Through the navel of night
And her dark eyelashes;

These lines are the owl
Hooting ominous messages
In choking pain
In pubescent twilight

Reminding man
Of the burden of being–
To wake to his blood and dust
In the scowling mist

Reminding man
The loaded canoe
Sails near the shoreline
Raw palm fruit causes cough.

Yesternight, the fourth masquerade
Danced the last steps
In the village square
In the dazzling klieg lights

And retired to Owu Bou–*
Every step a colourful memory
Every step a torrent of bliss
Beyond bugs and roaches.

Today, like every other day
This Olorogun* festive season
The fourth masquerade
Promptly stirs again

To chase and strike
Running, gasping, yelling mortals
Twitching on the edge
In their weakest moments, or glitches,

Not in the seething spleen
Of an avowed enemy;
In fraternal fanfare and fondness
To pluck overweening airs, from mortals

To rescue the hidden pearl
In the whirlwind of self, more so
After a frothy wine of power,
To delirious fans' applause

To hoist the halo of the land
Spawned by the silent mystery
Of fluvial spirits roaming
The imponderable swirling winds

The age-long rituals streaking with sap
In the foggy forests
The restorative sacrifices
At the riverside ...

O this Olorogun festival
Woven around the one with a stark dark face
Peripatetic, vicious, intractable
With a blazing cutlass in the sun

Sprouted from the loins
Of a sinewy feisty fish
Beyond the tiny size

Beyond the mystical glow

Aye's net caught
In far away Aghoro River
Hence the cognomen:
 Ala beni kolo kolo ...

And in steaming unison
The frantic fans tease it in mock song
Heightening the sportive ire
Floating scarily in the wind

And in steaming unison
The frantic fans tease it in mock ululation
Garnishing the tense splendour
Of the sun; stirring the blood of the fiesta:

> *Again, the masquerade will retire*
> *Without striking a soul*
> *Sankia, Owa ...*
> *Wúwú wúwú wúwú ...*

A little play ploughed into sweat
Bursts at the seams, harassing the hyacinths
Congregating on the shores
Of buzzing markets.

The wise utters little
Sinking into the smokescreen
The unreacheable depths
Of their homely skins ...

---

* Meeting-place of masquerades in the forest.
* The annual Olorogun masquerade festival of Ayakoromo, Delta State, Nigeria.
* The literal translation is "salt water is bitter", referring to the saline water of Aghoro River, and the viciousness of the masquerade.

Questions hang in the wind

Those who seek answers
To the whirling questions in the wind
Carry the earth's inveterate burden–
No sanctuary sprouts in a conundrum.

The burden of breath as wanderer
            In search of an anchor
            In the sealed scroll from on high
The burden of netted tilapias
            Exploiting entangled pathways
The burden of a woman's breasts
            Plunging us into crippling debts
The burden of phantom hugs
            Hiding the dagger of the mind
            In freezing fondness and fanfare …

The wind carries numb gestures
Of sadists and saints at crossroads
Of the racy dog
            Going past excreta
Of the exposed yam tuber
            No longer sinking in the soil
Of the carefree maggot
            Taking over the raffia palm

Of castrated compatriots
            Eyeing the juicy lap of nirvana
            On fallen bridges
Of the heedless masquerade
            Missing its steps
            In public glare
Of the tiny ants
            Of little moments

Growing into timeless pantheons–

A workshop for passionate star gazers
Whose duty, as they say,
Turns out a mere illusion
Or a smug exercise
Of some muggy passion.

O each step of sweat
On the inky staircase of solutions
To the knots of the mind
To the questions in the wind
Leads to more wandering and stillness
And sighs and yawns and moans
Howling in the horizon;

Living is an irredeemable abyss
A nameless nothing
Needing seasonless surfing and servicing
Like a playful cat, scratching
The earth's surface, for nothing.

And each step of penitence
Or rectitude or doxology
Springing from shallow depths
Only yields more questions
More complications, more sweat,
Like an entangled gold fish
Struggling in vain for freedom.

O come with me
To where a change of blood
Solves all riddles
Dogging the path
To the soul's satiation;
All mortal troubles
Spring from the blood.

The burden of blood

How can we enjoy laughter
On the wrong side of the mouth
Or hanging tremulous
On stung and twisted tongues
Between two canine teeth?

How can we enjoy laughter
When the burden of blood
Weighs us down a throbbing grave;
The fountainhead of true rapture
Still foiled by synthetic whirlwinds
Or rests, complacent,
On the margins of balking souls?

How can we enjoy laughter
When nuts tucked away
In sightless carapaces
Of clowns, remain uncracked;

When the brood of ancient hyacinths
A proteinous treasure trove
Buzzing with song, remains untapped?

This bald truth is the undying
Midwife of stillbirth suns
Living smudge of running waters;
The cannons, too, are dumb
Convulsing with the guilt of the land;
O how loud the gods speak
With the stinging voice of silence!

And our clan continues to cringe
Before importunate beings, who
Hold the yam and the knife

Who cause us to gasp and trip
A million times over, though
Not pursued, or even stalked
By the ubiquitous fourth masquerade.

Importunate beings who take the land
Not through fortuitous sleight
But by naked force; twisting
The fruity tale of stars
Congealing the blood of state.

O these importunate beings
Fly in the cosy air
In the warm bosom of the sun
Only to swoop on the public pouch
Down below, in breathless succession,
Like hawks having a free reign
On wayward chicks

Throwing around
abstruse scraps and shrapnel
Blinding dust and rust–
Catalysts of straying clans
Keeping the bard awake,
Beyond the dolphin
That sleeps with one eye open,
Constantly sleuthing,
Mustering men of munificence
Above the roaring tide.

No wonder even the dumb
Holler their praise names
In the kingdom of crooks;

This is the burden of blood
Unrepentant worshipper
In the frontierless shrine of flesh

Swollen suitor to dry winds
And that ominous flood pumping
Wanton waters into the stomach.

How can we crack
The riddle of the wretched
Spangled on a phony spectrum
Pandering to the lifeless toasts
Of a trillion lepers
Glued to sacred thrones?

The delectable flower
Welcoming invidious guests
At the balcony of her sunshine
Drops dead, without hope of a resurrection.

Only a madman
Thinks the wanton mangling
Of one's umbilical cord
In the market square
A hilarious spectacle,
Or, perhaps, the feathery caress
Of the passing wind.

Only a mad man shows off
The iron tethers on his testicles
As love gifts or, perhaps
A salute to the guts;
Hugging the strange men
Digging his grave– as if in a dream.

This is the unhealing wound
Of a rusty nail
Defying the balmy moats
Of tetanus injection
And deep-throated prayers;

This is the straight road
The anointed pathway
With branches and bends and barbs
Leading to life, in a stunted jungle.

O give this burden
A rightful name
Uproot its noxious suckers
With matching matchets and mattocks;

The okra tree, however tall,
Must bow to the whims
Of its indubitable owner
Along the corridors of the wind.

They need new names
(for El Rufai, nPDP & APC*)

They feign defection
From the homestead
Of sanguine dictators
Scribbling, or passing, glibly tongues
Through every strand of sunlight

To consummate their new names
On the substrates of the earth.

But just yesterday, and even today,
Our friends climbed spooky rafters
Of heathens, with pentecostal gusto
Their pockets bulging with arsenal
And the grand masters' direct lines

Thinking along
One straight line
Like Saul on the road to Damascus
Or the fourth masquerade
On the track of raucous fans
Or the pointed thing
Bared for fecund depths
In the enchanted grove
Streaking with sumptuous fluid ...

Now they feign defection
From the plundering party
To trap the halo of the moment
Clasping us to their breasts
Soaked in never-ending debts to their gods
Cringing us before our own shadows
Which scold us, like the continual baying
Of a rabid dog, at a haggard stranger.
This brand new birth

On the showglass of the times
In wilful harmony
With the green crowd
Tickles the gloating soul.

O we must make a statement
With burnt candles and dry inks
And shrunk physiognomies, in twilight
To hoist this apostasy, wanton,
On the flagpole of poetry.

We must make a statement
With the undying fibre of our voice
Echoing through the arteries
Of the dark void;
We must hold up sparkling words
As lampterns, to find a straight path
In this cocktail of murk.

We must trumpet this halo
Through the walls of the light years
Through distant oceans and fields.

We must screen the new names
Which wrap up ancient maelstroms
In fresh cocoyam leaves
For a priceless gift to the earth
Dour, like swirling smoke in moonlight.

We must paddle this heaving catch
Past swollen waves of the sea
Past hounds and bulldogs
Prying eyes of devious saints
And their double-decked munificence
In soft homely songs of the soul.

---

* Nasir Ahmad El-Rufai, a one-time Nigerian minister and author of
   The Accidental Public Servant.
* 'New' People's Democratic Party.
* All Progressives Congress .

They need new names II
(for EL Rufai, nPDP & APC)

The furrows or tongues
Of these new saviours
Tell nothing of dark-tanned dreams
In the damned mould
Of Saul's depravity–

Resplendent in outer make
Replete with inner crisis;
Reeking of the tomb's sore content.

O the cross of this age
Is the riddle of appearance
Carries us through long tedious tunnels
Burns out blood and bone.
The white sweat of the gods
Needs no handkerchief to dry up
Cancels out the strains of sunlight.

The bottom of this new name
Is in the enchanting melodies
Of the sunbird gleefully pecking
At red palm fruit
As if glued to the feast
In the forest of Amatebe

Where school boys
Played assorted pranks
Dodging to the town square
With no permit or exeat card
Now a broad highway
Hosting mansions and milestones
The wind, surely, is not static.

So why do the new saviours
Point to the rainbow
In the not-too-distant sky
Forgetting yesterday, when they
Pocketed the communal pouch
Blinking none of the six senses
Without sweat or contrition
Surpassing the penchant of their forebears
In the acrobatic mould
Of a monkey diving at banana?

O the limits of terrestrial lords
Is the starting point of benevolent gods,
Inviolate, cancelling out earthly plots
Even of those who need new names
To print same poignant designs.

Rage in the desert

(for Boko Haram*)

Terrorists taunt mortal blood
In the desert, like some plaything,
Perhaps a child's toy
Or the fourth masquerade
In the distant delta
Chasing and thrashing
Frantic fans, in blithesome strides.

The sweet breath of brotherhood
Stops in their flaming strikes
Flowing markets stall
In the smoky horizon
Dripping dreams hang
In the sulky sky
The soil too hot
For tender tendrils
In this feisty rage.

O the detached logic
Of power schemers
Who see human breath
As a mere off-and-on switch
Like the covert code
Of coven kings
Takes over the cringing earth
Replacing tingling crops
With tripping tombstones.

The enstranged lore
Of martyrdom dreamers
A handle for neutron bombs
In undecipherable gestures
Of the deaf and dumb

Smothers the world
To clear footpaths to paradise
In a seething one-sided fray
Stinging the sun in the scrotum.

Now the rusty rhetoric
From Aso rock*
Too enstranged to capture
The right mood
Loaded with abnegation
In a million toothless miracles
Flung on the insufferable masses
Too dazed even for manna
From the high heavens.

In this cadaverous night
When the moon mates
Hooded angels of darkness
From the far desert
Mountain freaks climbing for fresh air
Stumble on pointed stumps
Bandied about in sweet tongues
As fruit-packed shrubs and privets.

The few succulent fruits
From the rock
Are sucked dry, on their trees,
By sleepless saints
Boasting a handle for the desecrated
Only to consecrate the night
With vapid husks
Scorching sneezes and homing snarls.

---

* A militant Islamic sect in Northern Nigeria
* The seat of government in Nigeria

We hawk horrid memories

(for Boko Haram)

We hawk horrid memories
Of a sprawling landscape
To a listless world
Grappling with sundry stings
Staring at timorous time
Square on the weather-beaten tray
Of strange fancies spawned
By some dusky sage in the desert

Extending the shadow
Already too long and stifling
In the horizon, cast on mortals
By the masked moon.

Who on earth revels
In hawking loose beings
Whose rancid breath chokes the earth
Whose wild instincts
Defy all rational schools
Even in-house, without sap or dew
Swifter and more devious
Than a slithering cobra
On compromising branches?

Who dares sing bombastic songs
Before fresh corpses, saplings
Fallen to the cringing blast
Of Boko Haram bombs
Throwing around motley
Contortions and cracks
Misery and moans?

Let us salve the senses' errors
Make love anew, in the spirit
Of the creed of the moon
So we can pluck red nuts
From tall palm trees
In the summit of the sun.

Let us probe the masked moon
That deceived the straying cockerel
Into the depths of night;
Disarm her grinning antics
Or fall into the trap–
Except we smash the head
The wriggle of the wounded cobra
Is a steady sauce for suspicion.

O no need for mourners to rehearse
The moans of misery;
Do not listen to the prodding lines
Of wormy statesmen
Or hot-headed sages
The movement of the blood in brusque strides
Towards volcanic heights and broken pots.

Facing the flames
(for Boko Haram & their sponsors)

A palisade against
The roving light of the west
Held hostage by the incantations
Of mat-carrying initiates;

O drag them down
The mountain of shame
From where they pee
On messengers of the most high
In mythic flight–

The errors of the heart
Push benighted felons
To crooked endeavours.

The funerary drums begin to sound
In the depths of the desert.

Seize the wind
With bombs and bullets

Bellowed the surly voice
In the background
Rejected in the general count
Like a spurned suitor
Igniting furnaces of mass murder–
Whetstone of another war
On the back of a sullen loss.

We shall answer for
Every pint of blood
Shed on the trail
Of our fiery mouths–
Hollow in chastity
Without a compass, or circumspection

Pulling down caked clouds
On the homely drift.

O let this steely grip
By incensed green men, stay on
No pleas douse the resolve
To open their rancid entrails
In the centre of the market place;

When the swollen head crumbles
Stone faces behind
Grovel on the ground
Or take to their heels

And their vicious scheme
Of a sahelian drought
Across the land, hang
Without teeth, in the wind.

Let the priest of Odele*
Sanctify the surly horizon
Save this burning place
Of yet another black plot

To mate the menacing clouds
In the ripest season
Leaving behind
Howling offspring of carnage.

Legends of today

(for the 26 Bayelsa unemployed graduates)

The horizon erects statuettes
Of strange legends and lords
Who cruise the world round
In chartered jets and helicopters
In the swollen wings
Of floating white eagles;

The world below groans
In the frying flames of flow stations
And the long-drawn drought
Spawned by man's missed steps
Swallowing the soothing powers of the sun.

The horizon erects statuettes
Of strange legends and lords
Who block the free flow
Of oily props and peace of the soul
With their haughty breath
          Profane gestures
          Sunless signatures
Scanning every crowing voice
In broad daylight, for specks of dissent
Asking the weird question:

Who beats the drum in the forest?

These legends and lords
Survey our scrotums
Hounding and heckling us
With blustering uniformed men

On the streets
On cyberspace
On our phones

On our beds

For imagined, sharpened
Or obtuse threats
To the free reign
Of owls and bats and crows

Who cruise in weird winds
With heavy black blood
In their pouch and breasts
Choking every being to stupor
Forgetting the lion does not eat
A bestrodden animal.

If you must know, my lords,
Hunger beats the drum
In the rumbling stomach
Pumping up grit and guts
To cross those peevish paths
Pampered by the people's purse:

Don't we remember
When an orphan has a full stomach
He forgets his roots?

O the gauche paradox
Of blockheads and night men
Receiving scarce succour
From the coffers of the state
Gives teeth to the dictum
The Mami Wata takes life
On shallow shores.

And how sweet and discreet
Boro's* remains were exhumed
From the state of aquatic splendour
For a square earth to earth in his roots
So the ancestors woke up
To the strident sound of warriors' songs

Cannon shots and clash of cutlasses
In a colourful procession of canoes
Decked out in fresh palm fronds
And black-and-red costumes
At the riverside, tickling the waters
Silently flowing by; painting
The dews of dawn, in golden hues.

So the ancestors woke up
To savour the early morning breeze
Scented with the company
Of a sparkling kinsman,
Long in the rain ...

O let us look the way
Of lads carrying hurricane lamps
To find a path
In the long, grisly night,
Like striplings foraging for snail
In dark and damp corners;
Trudging with calloused feet
And dehydrated physiognomies
In clouded valleys
In the cold wind.

Let us look the way
Of Boro's extended offspring
In their suffocating corner of the earth
So they invest the capital
Gleaned through sappy sweat
On marshy, knotty roads
In saltless horizons.

What corpse, buried,
Leaves its legs outside?

---

* Isaac Boro, iconic Niger Delta revolutionary.

The triumph of charlatans

(for the new wave of Christianity)

Charlatans milling around the temple
Like akparakpa* fresh palm wine
Water down the salt of the earth
Besmear ancient sacred vestments
On the road to the moon
Open on infinite green fields.

Whose eyes are steady enough
To count the multitude of sterile stars
Roaming the pistillate sky?
O stretch not the goal post
      For lame prodigies to score
Stretch not your naked eyes
      Past the line on the pitch.

Purge your heart of heresy
      The sky has space
      For all flying things;
Purge your hand of horrid holes
      Looking for miracles in infernal corners;
Purge your eyes of lewd glances
      You may need to cut off that part
      To service the scriptures;
Purge your mouth of mendacities
      Tainted instincts do not fit into light.

The muse of modern man
On hallowed heights, is strange indeed,
Like the madman of Amatebe
Seizes the stomach-offering
Of neigbours, in open stealth
In the name of the Father

Proclaims nothing comes
Near their mouths
With bulging stomachs
And a rugged climb
To the summit of dreams

Planting demons in the whirlwind
To reap the expansive world–
Onions grow on cow dung;
A token of the blood of stone
Running through black veins
Sinking whole communes
With infinitely long throats.

Legends sprout from sweat
And the promise of bruises
In every conceivable field
Though the gods lubricate mortal paths
With morning dew that dries not
Until destiny's deal is done
In the infinite expanse of the sea
In wild wanton wavelashes.

---

* A kind of insect.

The wrong inheritance
(for the middlemen of the Creeks)

We step our solemn feet
On the bridge across raped seas
Bulbuls shriek in sultry daylight
In the surrounding forests
Knowing colourful masks
Hide this wild and weird world.

Spangled souls without a stake
In the affairs of loft
Whose voices sink in the vast sea
Like a tiny pebble
Are crowns of the coast
Inherit the choice estates
Infinite in their glow
Hosting man's baffling neons.

O who can cover the countless inanities
Glued to their mouths?
Who can carry this obese world
On their heads
And think they can lead
The choir in heaven;
The unheard music of delirium
Softly playing on the strings of their brains?

Nothing empty dissolves
Or swells or fossilizes
Even in the soulful touch
Of a damsel, even
In the most responsive regions
Of mortal physiognomy
Even in the navel

Of the mellow moon;

Something in the mould of being
Must grow or stand still or give way.

Something hooked by the heart
Fostered by travelling blood
That rocks the pointed point
Weaving waves in and out
Of buttered flesh
In the complicit closet,
Spreading warmest balm
On bleeding veins and joints
Like calm forests, after a bitter storm.

So something disqualifies
These seekers of peace
On the swirling waves of the creeks
Middlemen who dance on the graves
Of saints sacrificed in the struggle
Who take the lion's share
Of the proceeds of truce
Behind prying eyes

Nimble patriots who spit on
The lingering pains and spleen
Over unfulfilled prophecies
As fiendish and foolhardy
As squabbling landlords over territory
At my Agudama* backyard
Nibbling away, in secret triumph
Like the wraith-like Odidigboigbo*.

---

* An area in Yenagoa, Bayelsa State, Nigeria.
* One-time Governor of Delta State, Nigeria, Onanefe Ibori's praise name.

For Hamza Al-Mustapha*

The courts are a torn net
Hauled on the river; roving
Fish have a field day
Swimming through in shiny scorn;

Even the ones caught
Send a telepathic message
To their empathizing kindred
From the home-bound canoe
Through unyielding hyacinth

Not to mourn yet
Until they enter the pot.

---

* Chief Security Officer to Nigeria's one-time Head of State, General
  Sani Abacha.

No festivals here

Festivals have since recoiled
From streets along the waterway;
Dipped into rabid dungs of memory
Or buried in the overspilling clouds
Taken over the horizon
Scribbling the lean loves
Lining the age, like a kwashiorkor patient.

O what lascivious lies
Casting unbleachable coal tar
On overpowered stars–
Outcasts in deep congregation
Posing with seductive curves
In darkling corners of the earth

Swiftly abducting the godhead
With the fruity syllables
Of their hips or lips,
Hoisting flowery psalms
And spangled dreams
Like flying turtles in children's cartoons

Deepening strains of blood
Interlocked in the seething sky
Where midgets of men
Maul head-mountains
Or take them as footstool
Or, better still,
Image injectors, or projectors
With sprawling purses;

And the moon seems to place
A sentient seal
On this prickly paradise

Even without a hoot
The spirit of the age
Howling in the horizon
Ticking like a million minutes.

Here a full tide of oil
Breeds milky monsters at the top
Who taunt the treasury
Spitting sore slums and scraps
Though where the water pot stands
There is no dry season;

Burrowing in shrouded strides
Like the earthworm, king
Of the inveterate earth
Not a single bump
Though rooted against
A thousand breaths

Never faltering nor flattering
Like a smiling moon
On a forest-paved footpath at night
Egging the shadow on
To where hunger kills the soul
With a heaving petalled harvest
Hanging in the horizon.

This land stands on its head

We ring heavy church bells
As a consummate Catholic Catechist
Summons all to the Angelus
When the land stands
Giddily on its head

When steely snares
Woven into white depths
Hold mortals captive
In pithy dreams dead on the mind
Like a rabbit smothered in its hole.

Memory brings back dark entrails
Piled up in open interspaces
Of street corners and offices
In sly moods of bedrooms
And countless conferences.

O these stars in white smock
Who pamper the crucifix in public
Cloaking lewd laughters
In inner corners of the mind.

Swallowing up any spark
In endless stretches
Of potholes and puddles, dismembering
Wrinkled seventh-grade cars
In freezing tales of lost limbs
With no balm for the gash
And the air taut
Like a steel rat trap.

The snags of memory pile up
In the air, land, water

In loft jocund leaps,
Like laughing silver waves
Sliding high on the ocean
Before a licentious crash
Into the cataclysmic embrace
Of long-yawning mermaids.

Open paradox

This is the season
Of fleshy harvests
Portal of doughty dreams
And resonant laughters
Cascading down distant hilltops.

Yet the world below
Wilts in the heat
Of forlorn fancies
Sliding into morbid sorrow;
Countless mouths and stomachs
Lie fallow for ages,
Like ink-deprived pens
That cannot write.

This is the season
Of cerulean skies and placid seas
Even in the presence of incensed gods
And lost sojourners find their way
To the main market
In swiftly sailing canoes
Like snakes slithering away on water.

Yet the economy of aborigines
Shrinks in dire thraldom
In long laborious labyrinths
Baring the smudge
Of soot on the white smock
Of coast dwellers, paddling

On the margins
Of their own oily swamps,
Like the strange dilemma
Of a gleeful bride

On the back seat
In her own nuptials.

Or the damsel in delectable apparel
Who strummed soulful songs on the podium
To a roariously doting crowd
Only to fall to a sword
In an ante-room, without a row.

The howling wind

No one can tell
The colour of the wind
Even in its Christmas paraphernalia
Like the heart
Of some darkling god
Open to the prognosis
Of some pukka prophet.

The colour of the supreme
Resonates in the howling
Fanfare of the wind
The milky sea breeze
The ruthless lightning and hurricane
The pungent squawk of thunder …

O the wind can tear
Mountains apart
Shatter the rocks …

The undecipherable gestures
Of the I AM THAT I AM
Of the earth and sky
Activate tardy elements
Like a genial blonde
Manly parts which puke
Where they eat;
Like the prophecy of the bard
Sets dying suns on fire.

In her sensual caress
The wind gathers
Hidden secrets of the sea
In a swirling maelstrom
In the mermaid's den

Sends same in instalmental folds
To the jocund bosom of the Boss.

O the rustling river
Of flowing legends
Their sumptuous fluids
Powered by the wind
Leading to the eternal godhead
The funerary traps and iron dams
No power dares break or barricade.

Leaves sway their wet waists
In the rapturous rainy season
In love tango with the wind
Bearing vermillion fruits
Carrying the incandescent burden
Of a squinting squire
Condemned to meandering paths or ways
Or muffling altars or temples.

Does man know
The same wind sails
Flailing mortals in the dry season
Distributing acrid desert dust
To every naked nostril
When all nature shrivels

Like a dehydrated cholera patient
Failing to float leisurely
In the blue sky
Like the squeaky kite,
Like a burst balloon?

Fate of man

Globules of triumphant blood
Gurgle in a swelling heart
Wading through boiling waters
And neutron bombs
Shaming the brittle barricade
Of hurricanes and howitzers.

When mortal blood tastes triumph
It walks like a royal priest
Demons and capones and their ilk
Do obeisance to a divine staff of office
The world watches the spectacle
In wanton wonder:
The racing canoe never sails backward.

The blood of a triumphant heart
Climbs veins and arteries posthaste
Tickling mortal brains and bums;
The dead live beyond triumph

Beyond fantasies and fables
Beyond bush fires and burning gods
Beyond rodents and man
Bumping into one another
Scampering for safety
From smothering sanctuaries

Beyond iron traps and flinching fields
Fleeing monkeys squalling in treeless forests
Beyond the mutant chameleon
Which can not wait to ingraft
The colour of the flames

Beyond the billowing wiles

Of conquistadors and capones
Blowing man to squalid slums
The frothy waves of sludgy seas
Roaring in their guttural voices
In the distant horizon
Slapping eagerly waiting shores
With their towering heights;

The blistering sunlight overwhelms
The howling wind, the sultry birds
In forlorn feverish flight.

In this vast world

The dripping grace of their gods
Swells their pouches and powers
Tramps translate into inviolable titans
Beckoning lustily to covetous souls
To wear a haughty crown of thorns
Or serve in servile stations forever more.

The tongues of ancient gods
Spit fire and brimstone and hailstone
From the tawdry world of the dark
Oblivious of the overwhelming ardour
Of the white light, the cornerstone
That props up the horizon.

In this vast world
Parrots can be silenced
Winging lions hobbled
Tall dreams dwarfed or stunted
By the pithy power of magic coins
In morbid league
With a *babalawo*'s chants
Or the manoeuvring of heartless covens.

In this vast world
Hordes of Giants
Take the broad way in stealth
Licking wild salt alone
Without flight in light
Leaning on
Dysfunctional wings
Of fallen gods.

May thunder release
The muffled manhood of the masses

In a meteoric flight to the moon
In the simultaneous echo
Of seven primed cannons–

The hen's sickness
Never tarries till evening;
The foliage of freedom is ever fresh
In the silhouetted forest
Of shrivelling thorns and cactus.

The child can pluck the moon

With a sanguine stretch of the mind
A child can pluck the moon
From the sky's socket
And unseen lions and leopards
Escort the toddler conqueror home
Before baying hounds
And sulky soldier ants.

The earth is intrepid without dreams
Sinking down in smutty depths
Or long overarching clouds
To rise winsome on the podium
In soft stirring songs
For soothing flowers and pecks.

O the coast is not always fair
The early birds may not
Sleep on the beach
The bone that tans the teeth
Gives problems to the tongue.

Do we need reminding
Where there is no eseni*
Agbọgịdị steals the show of the pot?
When a hen loses a fight
The owner shrinks in shame?

When the soothing song
Of the soul is slaughtered
By morbid man or beast
Or even the elements
The world goes dumb,
 Like a bruised drum

The salt of the sea is drowned
In the cadaverous calvary of waves.

In the frigid breeze
Standing still in the horizon
Summoned at the break of dawn
Palm fronds from the sages
Shunned by the priest
Of the wilting grove
The bleeding dove flapping its wings
Against the sombre oracle ...

We wake up in the delta
To sweltering flow stations
And oil wells colouring
Free flowing waters
The earthy blaze
And greasy chemicals
Covering the moon's face
Harassing the deep green herbage
Wilting tender tendrils

Strange as the laughter of lepers
In a depraved colony
Angling for ineffectual apothecaries
Straining for the soul's flight
Even to synthetic hills.

Naked in the sun

Under the unction
Of some heinous god
Layabouts sit before a set table
Winking at the hilltop
Where the living petals of dream
Are dug in muddied rungs.

Out of the fetid air
Of some tyrant's kingdom
Sprouts a garden of greenery
Where farmers plant with songs
Tendrils shoot out in endless acres
Without the fecund touch of rain
Clouds bring loud laughters
Though the horizon is overcast

For those who sow mortal blood
On slaughter slabs, like red tomatoes
On cursed soils, behind the whistling wind

Out of irksome crossroads
Behind the baring sun
Open only to culprits
Come preachers of platitude
Yes, they proclaim continence
Like Binebai's* seventh virgin
Though exuberant in their pants:

The smell of dried shrimp
Or pounded rotten crabs
Gravitates crawling thing
Even in the dead of night
The smell of camphor
Wards off crawling things

The smell of mythylated spirits
Helps veinous cramps ...

Out of a half-hearted combat
With unyielding gods
Behind cloggy shrines
Comes stars afflicted
By the preening pus
Of fanatics and sycophants
Swelling by the second

Leaving livid scars in the wind
Burying incandescent stars;
Self-seeking souls in sullen tempers
Festooned in saviour's robes
Yielding nothing salutary
Only ash and hogwash

---

* Ben Binebai—a Nigerian playwright and scholar.

Song of innocence

Our memory is reloaded
With the laughter
Of moon-lit evenings
On the lap of granny's endless tales
Fresh and luscious as dewdrops
Sleeping with deep green vegetation overnight.

O the cleansing of the beginning
Granny's shadow lurking behind
Every step or speech or sentiment
At the foot of the almond tree
Flamboyant in its dark green foliage
In receding evening light.

The steepy mountains
We climbed every single second
In the spongy horizon;
The scary footholds, hanging
On natural ropes
Growing wild across trees,
Like passionate monkeys;
The dizzy solitude in sundry heights
Burning with fierce fervour
Burning out the strain
Of the daylight sun ...

O shield our noses
From the dust of the midday horizon
The natural plots sewn together
In the impenetrable harmony of mists
Riding the apocalypse
With dragon's breath;

Shield us from
The cat's silent steps
In the belly of the night
The robber's cautious shadow
The point of no return*

Shield us from
The psychedelic distractions
Of whitewashed damsels
Dazzling like winged beings on high
The melting pot of the heart
Planting riots even
In the blood of the blind.

---

* The Gold Coast Castle in Ghana, West Africa – a seaside fortress
used for slave trade by the British in the 17th century. There is the
notorious "Point of no Return" which was the outlet where slaves
who were able to withstand the rigidity of their confinement were
shipped to intended destinations.

Dunamis

Now drunk
On the putrid urine of power
Their true form takes flight
Cruises to the naked fore
Blocks the majestic fall
Of fecund rain, on human folk.

Like smoke that has swallowed
The ubiquitous liquor of wind
Sways this way and that
They float without meaning in the air;

O none so saintly
To disband this howling self-system
Surrender the self-spoiling
Spoils of almighty dunamis
For communal indulgence;
None so saintly
To shun its stunting seeds
Shame the general hunger
Harrying the horizon.

Yet they stand on the podium
Before the moaning masses
Their sturdy hopes
Mowed down by the caterpillar
Of their rancid wits
Waving magic wands in the wind
 Those loaded dividends ported
To the four corners of the earth
In absolutely abstract terms
Open only to compromised eyes.

They curse the very thought
Or divination, or saucy slogan
Seeking to deprive
Saints a second season
With the sacred key of life
On mountaintops,
To unlock the stubborn moon.
Afterall, Oleilei* remains
On the beautiful beach.

Nothing shows the moon
Loathes this weird company
Laughter lavishly sprouting
From her genial bosom
Oblivious or crassly indifferent
To the restless tongue of fire
Licking up earth's dire foliage.

---

*   a bird.

Rhythm of the forsaken

The world is incensed
When spurious saints snuggle
Into the moon's bosom
Drunk on the people's tonic
Taking a heady leap
In the village square
Though like the frog
However incensed cannot bite.

From the distant cradle
This world pees
On love's lofty canvas
Doves wobble in spunky flight
Wounded wings hanging
In dire throats
Choked by twisted canons
Of the black power game
Criss-crossing the clan.

O no pee scents
On the substrates of the earth–
Even the salty pee
Of turbid saints;
No dark plot passes for
The queen of the night
Fondling naked senses.

These saints draw
Their chiselled swords
From glittering scabbards
With plastic caresses
Smiles without depth, or anchorage
Floating on the soppy

Belly of the horizon
Like crude oil on water
Canceling the sizzle of the sun.

Yet marionettes mount
The manic moon
Here and there
Without a compass
Without smug blustering godfathers,
Without a crutch ...

Here and there
Marionettes mount the moon
On the staircase of raw guts
Humming the soulful song
Of stirring birds
On the corridors of dawn
Chirping and chanting salty lines
In squally storms
And horrid hurricanes
In the infinite flight of wings

The pedals of hollow wind
Surge on the spirit
Of the forsaken;
Inner fire burnishes cast-iron wills
Cascading through rustic groves and squalid seas
Into canons that nourish mortal blood.

The death of dark memory

All mortals relish
The death of dark memory
Looking for wedges
To cover leaking canoes
Stitches to hide hideous nakedness
In seasons of studs and sighs.

A flourishing memory
Perfumes the senses
Eternal songs, they rock
The inner being
Climbing the staircase of blood
To the precincts of the pithy sun
Alien to craggy bones
Suffused in intrepid memories.

O sweet strands of memory
Hosts of radiant angels
Sow teeming harmonies in the wind
Alien to discordant dark contours
The voluptuous clouds
Sitting on the horizon;

The fourth masquerade
Must pursue doting fans
With a glistening cutlass
In resplendent regalia
In eye-catching strides.

Sweet strands of memory
The salty spume of the sea
Colour of the inimitable carnival
Winsome melody of the mind
The senses gallop in their lewd sockets

Like gusty excited horses
Dispelling the groggy myth
Of grey hair and wrinkles.

And I remember
The unassailable lore of the land:
The fish in biran's* company
Exudes the same buoyant aura

An unflagging star with a stuttering start
Can seize the season, like Serena slam
Like a stammering thunderbolt.

---

* A kind of fish

Silence is not golden

The choir of silence
Dampens the fire of the soul
In the dingy tropics
Strangulates salubrious laughter
By the scruff of the neck

Greying hearts need the window
Of rainbow voices;
The bleating sheep courts
Food for the silent.

O though unseen
Dark dots tan human breath
Like Hausa kola the teeth;
Distil the kernel of things
With clairvoyant words, or
Leave the horn of the soul
Grovelling in a dungeon
Exploding at the long last
With a massive voice
Like seven cannons in one stride
Freeing the frozen world.

Besotted souls shout to the sky
Scavenge for non-existent winds
In the scattered horizon
For a free flight to fame;
Only a moron beats his chest
In front of genial in-laws–
Advertising wanton bravado
To seek their seal.

O sink with a loud voice
Into the swallowing soil

Like the strident blood
Of a slit cockerel;
We tread on gold, without knowing
Without even a synthetic grin
Forged in the wind.

Wake those dormant senses
Into a formidable voice in the wilderness
Into the ecstasy of triumph
Sailing swiftly on salted winds
Tickling splintered memories
Of dane guns and cutlasses and cudgels.

Perverts on the prowl

The slur of a stolen mask
From the forbidden rafters of owu bou*
And the fatal strike
Of infant souls in Potiskum*
In the dewdrops of dawn
Signpost a perverted clan;

O these soulless felons on the prowl
Even in sacred corners of the world ...

In the profane pilfering
In the dead of night
And the wanton massacre
Of nameless souls
We weave a mat of bankruptcy
For our multiple stakes
As star inhabitants of planet earth

Stripping ourselves naked
In the market place
In the broad light of day
Heaping an abominable
Dump of shame
On savvy sires, interminably
Tied to the womb

For the wounds of despoliation
Find even the unseen foetus
Pull the curtain on the lighted road;
O descant the darts of darkness
From the conspiracy of masks
Culpable witnesses to the purloining bond
Muffled sighs sailing in the wind.

O let the turgid souls
On the sirened seat
Who puke where they eat
Like a primed penis
Step aside for the suppressed
Salt of the earth
Waiting in the winds
Or be stripped of dire carapaces;
Garish cascades, visionless oracles
Carrying a pile of unanswerable queries
On their vague heads.

How can the sun prosper
Without uncluttered light
Radiating her footsteps?

How can the moon
See through knotty pathways
In pitch darkness
Eyes completely closed?

How can we summon the breeze
For her warm caress,
Or motherly balm,
Bruised to the last bone?

---

* Meeting-place of masquerade groups in the forest
* In July, 2013, gunmen, suspected to be Boko Haram Islamists,
  struck in a Government Secondary School in Mamudo, Yobe State,
  Nigeria, killing several children.

Give us sanctity

And if we seek to see
The awesome nakedness
Of some sulky god
Gushing tides will swallow
Already shrinking foreshores
In one snap of its yawning jaws;

Unseen detonators will
Grate on the horizon
Like the mystical massacre
In a lonely ambush
Of state security hounds
Stalking the ombatse *cult.

Yet in sober truth
Even the deadliest god
Is far cleaner in sum
Than a self-consecrated church–
Sullen and implacable in spirit
Slick and regal in flesh
Crushing the blind folks
On their mental slate.

O give us sanctity in the wind–
The first fruit of the godhead
Not luxuriant signs
And wondrous derring-do;
These can be sourced from without
Even from claws of lions
Or a vulture's bald head–
Totems of some cruel god,

When invoked in nakedness
Cockerel in hand
In some awning darkness.

Gives us life

When men mount
The dizzy heights
Of a garlanded throne
They hobnob with birds and bats
In the boundless stretches of the horizon
And fantasize about romance
In the sappy sun and sister planets

Stumbling into the patriots' petitions
And the strident clamours
Down below, in a distant haze.

Give us bakeries, not daily bread;
This can breed another stretch of inconstancy
Buttered with a rousing round of rhetoric
Like Power Holding Company of Nigeria
So we lean on naked sweat
Not their flickering senses.

Give us tarred roads
Like tarmacs at Nnamdi Azikiwe Airport*
So we can cruise
To fecund farms far away
With brimful energies
And feisty spirits
To cut down giant mahoganies;

Not malfunctioning caterpillars
Showcased on patched paths
Putrid potholes and puddles
On which commuters rock azonto*
Spawning countless miscarriages.

O give us virgin doves
To decorate the horizon
So night can sleep
With both eyes closed
In the clasping bosom of life;

Not with nagging mares
Mutating dreams
To horrid fantasies
Not the laughter of fear
Nor the fear of laughter
Fouling the obsequious air.

Give us drums and sticks
White frocks and handkerchieves
So satiated dancers
Can evolve into living stars
So lame spirits can have
A smooth climb to the moon;

Not dancers without the giddy
Magic of the waist,
Floating in the numb air,
Without soul or bone,
Like children's animations.

---

* Nnamdi Azikiwe International Airport, Abuja, Nigeria
* A kind of dance

The bankrupt mind

These masters of masks
Pull wild strings
From those high cliffs
Twisting mortal paths,
The canyon of livid mushrooms
And thorns and cactus
Yet so close to the skin.

Unhidden, like a sonorous snore
In darkness, they pay their debts
In funerary bristles, bungling airs
Sowing skinny barns
In far away anthills
In the minds of mortals
Squabbling over loading bay
When all boats are leaking.

And again, in the cloak of night
In measured feline steps
They offer a sullen bowl
Of blood and beasts to their gods,
Like a feast of ants on sugar
The sweetness enters their heads.

They paddle robbers and murderers
Free of charge
To their victims' sanctuaries
To profane pearly peace.

O a funeral is never distant
Wherever the scene, the loss of breath;
A funeral is never a jubilee
Though animated with cascading fanfare–
Wherever the scene, the sullenness of shadows

The soberness of another lost battle.

The bankrupt mind
Is like a drunken eye–
Sees seven in giddy delirium
Beyond flesh or form or film;
The slapped eye sees stars
Dancing in the morbid air,
Incandescent, with multiple sparks

Flummoxing sight, sap, and snares
Building dykes and drainages
In the turning space
On the brink of intractable flames
Until the saviour's second coming.

This is the steely trap
Saints must jump over
Or abandon the call
Dismembered in their native communes
Scattered in lost tracks
Like a lunatic vending nothing valuable.

The delta of yore

When memory takes you
On a cinematographic voyage
Through dew-draped forests of yore
Phosphorescent bubbles
Walk gaily through your blood
Teasing the tearful eye–
Harbinger of celestial things.

Animated squirrels on the crest
Of virgin palm trees
Pecking at their luscious red fruits;
Euphonious songs of the canary
Tickling the humid horizon
In the unfurling sun;
Antelopes in squelching strides
Ravishing flourishing green fields ...

Now the air is taut
Like a steel antelope trap
Ready to snap ...

And we take strange steps
Deeper and deeper into the woods
Or some irredeemable trenches
In combat with seven dreaded spirits
Intangible, knotting the gurgling blood
Ruling foul forests of the clan.

The gods have stricken us
With a bizarre ailment:
Immutable bondsmen
To insensate strangers
On oily seats, who perforate
Even the raw breath

Mortals take for naught.

These strangers,
Not in an aboriginal sense,
Pedantic strangers to lofty seats
Without tools, without
Dulcet propositions,
Masters of musty gestures
Now treated as wistful patriots
Carriers of the white light,

Strip us of divine glow
Strip us of luscious laughter
Echoing in the vast greenery
Hanging in far away hills.

O let the edenic memory
Of the Delta of yore
Speed our steps over
These fixed crosses
These slippery paths of stone–
Stunning incendiary felons
To the bone.

O let us see
Their frantic fangs
Drop with red-hot speed;
Let the mischievous wind blow
So we see the anus
Of the secret laughters
Of priests and barons and cultists and politicians
Spawning mournful moments as milestones.

The new stars

We can hear the chants of victory
Echoing in the distant hills
Blazing banners heralding the arrival
Of that gawky godfather
His stomach sputtering sticky grime
His weighty winds rustling
Through the torrid horizon.

We can see the wings clearly now
Visible even from the lowest valley
Fanning the unfailing cycle
Of miscarriages and stillbirths
In concert with grisly gods
Gnarling the grim air
Discolouring the rainbow long ripe
In the belly of the sky
Bungling new routes to the waterfront

Where magic hawks perforate
The prurient pouch of memory
Their secret steps shame the cat's
Their ferocious pounce shames the leopard's
Bulldozing through sacred barricades
With hot, hot claws

Plundering the public flesh
With flaming gusto
Hoisting the skeleton on a flagpole
For the universal eye, frightened
To a dead corner, like an escaping rat.

But we reap heaving harvests
In the middle of a maelstrom
Silently striving triumphant

Even in the midst of barren fields;
Diamonds hide in fleshy depths
Tugging at the substrates of human guts
To reap their stupendous bounties.

Swollen shoulders scratch the surface
Of the wind, rattled by its hollowness;
Shrinking guts in moments of crisis
Gather nothing, rattled
By nightmares and tumbling dreams.

The road to fate

Carrion-crows in ritual dance
Around the oozing carcass
Signing mournful signatures in the wind
Remind man of his fatal limits.

The road to the market
Buzzes with people
Higgling and haggling over
Moods and merchandise
Promising, like a budding rainbow.

The road to the cemetery
Wears a sullen sackcloth;
The eerie stillness of the air
The morbid shriek of owls and bats
The disconsolate tears on the tomb
Spell man's ultimate sanctuary.

O no garland on this road
Banishes the hazy chill
Hanging in the horizon;
The soulful sound of siren
Carnivals floating in the air
For seven long days
Closing roads, streets and cities
Only hoist the hole in the heart
Print the wounded blood in the air,

How can pageantry or glee
Heal the gash
Even apothecaries exacerbate?
No quantity of water can quench
The roaring flames of Jesse-Ogube*
Swelling by the second with flowing fuel.

A clown departs the stage
Through a bizarre back door
Hiding dates of burial;
The blast of multiple cannons
Heralds the passing of capons

Shaking the entire universe
To her roots, in the precincts
Of a withering moon–
The victim of this wormy curse
Eating up the sap of the earth
Bit by bit, into a tombstone ...

Out of breath
The pursuing fourth masquerade
Remembers the prize of penitence
But already, the human race
Has sunk irretrievably
Into the bland confines
Of mass discoloration.

---

* A community in Delta State, Nigeria.

On human relations, dreams & the gods

Do not prostrate before the moon
Or present oblation to the clouds
To paste your dreams
On the purlieus of the sky;

There is no solitary passage
To the ornaments of the world.

The fanfare of the fourth masquerade
Swells with fans straining
And gasping for breath
On the long expanse
Of the town square

Swallowing all mortal inhibitions
Or boundaries of blood
With no side acquiescing
Without a show of stamina;
An evenly tempered relationship
Is the centre of the world.

Who says the solitude of self-seekers
Who revel in cowing comrades
Pushing kinsmen to obscure corners
Like a drenched hen,
After the season of harvest
After the awesome mask
No longer adorns the face
Is no cause to caress the crowd
In the fullness of floods
In the fullness of festivals
In the fullness of offices?

The mistakes of blood
And the heart
Blindfold susceptible human folk
Down the abyss; without
Milestones or monuments
Without footprints or signposts.

Yet some expired maestros regale us
With craggy phallus and orifices
Long lost their friction, in high life
Mating wild clouds on the sky
Begetting weird offspring
Timeless scar of mauled moments,
Like a leopard's hapless victim.

O sainthood and sacrifice serve as dew
To human dreams and fancies
Yielding clear vibes and visions
Leading to prized diadems
Birdsongs seizing the horizon
In climes standing on two legs.

Dark stars

We must count the stars
On five leprous fingertips
We must count these stars
On scattered teeth
Of shrivelled corn cobs.

We must count the stars
Which bring down multiple mists
Upon the clan at the break of day
When nests open their dew-draped doors
To the world in throaty songs

Celestial beings with broken wings
Cannot carry pregnant messages
Through the open skies
To retrieve lost moments
Of the earth;

The legendary cheetah
Without those elastic legs
Cannot be a speedster;

A broken burglary proof
Loses the shielding power
Of a brooding hen
Over her tender offspring,

Like tongues of fire
In harmattan shrubs
Drive away wild beings
In the dead of night.

Patriotism parades a perfumed name
Like Givenchy, not the leprous air
In climes under the tropical skies;

O do not think
Only maestros washed with herbs
Or washed by ubiquitous mermaids
See beyond the moment's dimness.

Come let us toast
To whitewashed patriots of our day
Who beat hefty chests
Before disillusioned in-laws
To remove specks in their eyes
Long grown symptomatic mucor

Only to falter in every step
Ringing a dumb bell
At the very moment of reckoning.

Unrepentant, like the python
In unimpeachable grip of its prey
These patriots have drained all eggs
Across the dumb clan
Even before the break of day
Scattering empty shells in the horizon.

The wide road

They give you the watchword
Of the secret road to Jerusalem:

> *Patronize whitewashed covens*
> *Or remain low in the spirit.*
> *Our meetings spew raucous songs*
> *And long fraternal doxologies*
> *Offering the wise ones of the altar*
> *Perfumed paths to the peak.*

No argument thrives here
All dọbalẹ* to the high command
In the mould of Fela's zombie
And clowns get magisterial crowns
And the holy strike of thunder
Prolongs the people's pains
In the terrestrial world.

Here I ring the bell of bards
Who see through the sparkling garments
And tawdry smiles of musketeers;
You do not bury a dog
To consummate a clean plot;
You do not shed intimate blood
To potentiate a pure spirit–

A crass cannibal cannot be a godhead.

No wonder
Whoever courts the mystery of Egbesu*
Must present a white petition–
The white cloth has no hand
In the massacre of blood brothers

Not even a distant mortal
Not at crossroads with the light
Or out to mortify the white race–
A white heart needn't fear
The mystery of the white cloth.

So the white symbol
All over the universe
Dreads oil, stands above
The cabalistic crowd
Roving in volcanic summits
Above blood-sucking sophists
Who pull down the inveterate earth
On whitewashed altars.

---

*   Yoruba word for bow; genuflect; prostrate.
*   Ijaw god of war.

A loud homily

A contrite thief treads softly
Even with a masked visage;
For pilfering adventurists
On some garlanded throne
Contrition floats on the mind
Like a long dead log.

For pilfering adventurists
On some garlanded throne
Contrition is a lifeless word
Consigned to lexicons long forgotten,
Or offering quiet service
To loud sanctimonious hymns
On some insignificant altar.

O the blind does not miss
The covert covenants
Of the salt of mankind
Who openly spit
On the narrow way;

The blind does not miss
The blistered spores of the soul
Scattered on endless meadows
Even the upturned honour
In high quarters
Shining on the earth
Through acquiescent interspaces
Like sunlight, when the day
Stands on its head.

The blind does not miss
The throbbing tapestry
Of pliant pilgrims

Floating faiths
Creepy hosannas
Surface grimaces

Imprecise moorings
On the ever-swelling river of want
Watching a rightful glory
Abscond in the crashing waves
Of the vast, vast sea
The fruitless tip-toeing
To reach fleshy racks
Planting wormy pains
In the substrates of the heart
The pile of unanswered prayers
The mangled mountains
Encircling God's shapely image ...

And who says
It is of consequence
How we clamber
To the summit of the earth?

O carry the soul along
In loud self-umbrage–
The living insignia of breath
After the carapace
Is returned to dust
Imprinted on the pages
Of man's terrestrial sojourn
In naked light, or in some
Secret corner of the globe.

Remember, long guns
And detonators and pranks
Have one morbid target:

To kill the soul
In uncluttered morning dew
When the forests wake
From yesternight's slumber
In creamy green suits.

The patriot's compass

The true tickle is in the heart
Where the moon finds a field
To stretch its steady luminescence
Beyond the limits
Of an unyielding night.

The true tickle in the heart
Sprouts from the mellow
Orifices of memory
In the staircase it unfurls
For kindred spirits to consummate
The crowns of their hearts

And the elements come together
Gregarious in their green creed
Etched on the lap
of a flowing stream

Not minding the spoils of office
And their wondrous estates
Beclouding insufferable remembrance
Of yesteryears of wet garri
And groundnuts or palm kernel
Bursting forth from barren bones
And burnt out blood.

O how we tread softly
On this vast globe
On the fearful prospect
Of drowning naked
With six-inch blocks
Tied to the waist
Wobbling with stuck breath
In deep deep waters

Without even an imaginary straw
For the crisis-laden soul
To clutch at.

Vultures cross the mental horizon
Flapping wet wings, in ominous knowledge
Of the password to hell;
And swallows and eagles,
Not to be outdone,
Fly around the mind
Shrieking in pregnant relish
Like a kingdom's elated spokesman
Announcing a long-delayed coronation.

So the shadow which domiciled
In the forlorn horizon for ages
Scours the soul for swallows and eagles
Disappears in the awesome canvas
Of the rainbow in the near distance.

Rising above the tide

The mistake in destiny's map
Carries certified tramps in frenetic tides
Toward a crown of needles
And a teeming conundrum

Toward a mass of green vegetation
Transmuted into a brown cellar
O man's tremulous moods!
It is not for nothing, comrades
Dolphins sleep with one eye open
The crocodile is blind to colour.

Like the Iguana, they do not have ears
For wild gossips or moans or murmurs
Nor for the haunting tremors of wetlands
Nor for the teasing taunts of true stars
Nor for the alternative toasts of sages
Who dive far into the deep
For pearls tucked away
In the bosom of inveterate mermaids.

O how their ears angle
For pandering fables
From the mouths of benighted fans
Painting tingling pictures on their mind
Like the early garden of Eden
Like the manatee which tickles
Its hapless preys to death.

O let the wide world
Go for a cleansing
Of the innermost strands of the soul
At the sacred waterfront
So the queen of the night

Can send her sensuous perfume
To all corners of the earth
Heaving with too much selves
Nude and sleep-walking
In the dark, for too long.

This earth needs sunlight
In her innermost chambers–
The heart, together
With elemental prayers
To rise above the tide
That is neck deep
Evolve a new foliage
In the steaming horizon
Over the remaining seasons.

Not soulful isolation
Masquerading as contentment–
The goat that avoids yam
Has a broken set of teeth;

Not souls strained in the blood
In fresh morning dew
Parading as the chosen ones–
A frightful apocalypse
In garments of promise.

These yawning omissions

These yawning omissions
Under the tropical skies
Perforating the loft canvas
Of our own creeds;

The detached plugging of holes
Pretentious baring of hearts
On the podium of public glare
Parodying Hannah's sobbing beauty.

Let this cross pass over:
The silent shadows of scavengers
On the walls of a flummoxed fate
Riding on ghostly dreams;

The entrails of insidious godfathers
Veiled in scented habiliments
Forgetting the tide of today
Is far too strong
For their frail bones
Far too fast
For their frail brains ...

This brood of fugitive hawks
Bereft of benign blood
Strike a double leap in the wind
A double boon in the tide
Aided by mystics and masters and mermaids;

Seeds of sunlight
Do not grow
On cloud-caked hearts
Forests inhabited
By diabolical tropical gods.

O the cringing nerves of aborigines
Paddling across seven seas, hiding
A million sharks, sweating
In the moon making their day
For blood calls to blood
In the deafening strike of thunder.

Who on earth can comb
The roving substrates of a storm
Impregnable, scattering all across its way?
Who on earth can boast anchorage
For a depraved soul and his sword
Smothering even the altar
Of the most high?

Who on earth can clip the wings
Of the corpulent crow and carrion
Having wilfully seized the wind?

How can the bard lament
The bars of a rosy race
Sinking into smudged depths
Beyond the punting pole
When the world
Surges gingerly forward?

The kingdom of self-seekers

No one stumbles on
Deadly spirits in feisty glee
In the bowels of Ndoro Bou*
In the unfathomable depths of the night
And scurries away
Without a scar.

The music of mystic birds
Play in guttural cadences
In the background
Flapping shadowy wings
In the horizon ...

Sometimes, whatever befalls us
As mortals, comes from the self
Even the strike of the fourth masquerade;
Disillusioned initiates, rueing their fate,
Rake up dry bones of memory

Scattered across several seasons
Splintered time-bombs planted in the psyche
Exploding at the height of consciousness;
Smashing the unborn mortal
On long uterine walls, in anguish,
Without as much as a swan song.

The harmony of satiated souls
Sparks in the strides of time
The salt of stillness
Agrees not with hot-headed broods

Drowns the senses in flight
Beyond inward winds
Resplendent in sight

Rotten in the innermost sites.

O see the wanton cracks
In the kingdom of self-seekers–
Covert, inconstant, in form and frame,
Which accepts no kola nut
For a truce; no palm wine
For violent surges on the sea

The passing wind hollering
Her hollow brims
Extending long green fields
Lying fallow without end
Or falling for coy scabs
On the naked beachsand
In the scorching heat
From the punctual oven
Up on the sky.

---

* The forest of Ndoro, Bayelsa State, Nigeria, is reputed to have
spell-binding mystical powers.

On the media, intellectuals, and marabouts

The media and intellectuals too
Are no longer subtle accomplices;
They now carry acidic arsenal
Across open spaces
To the doorstep of partisan foes,

Sprawling like roaring waters
In the deep spumy sea
Or an overarching army
Encamped at the city gate
Ever ready to pounce–
So resplendent in a dismal way.

The new patriots pad their path
In their breasts, together
With throbbing marabouts;
O these ghoulish marabouts
Quartered in secret hovels
With occultic hair
And white-chalk-circled eyes
Cover background interspaces
And exposing pores–

More ubiquitous
Than the wind's breath ...

And the shallow songs of heathens
Swallow the soulful choir of the cherub
On whose canvas sparks heavenly memories
Their long throats wet the ground
So crowns fit the head of clowns;
The clan, distraught, lives through the loss
Dawns come and go
Without the warm touch of light.

No one tries the patience of Odele*
For too long, like those wanton lads
At boarding school, tying
A friend's fleshy thing and scrotum
During siesta on a double-bunk bed
With a long rope, drawn and released
At the other end, in turn
Softly remembering the conundrum
Of squirrels caught with
Wire traps and palm fruits.

 No mask made by man
Hides the twisted contours of a face
In broad daylight, for too long;
Not even consummate crooks
Who bamboozle blood brothers
Or provide ready tinder
To true comradeship
Exploding in hearty flames.

This lair of bearded prophets
Inconstant in colour, like the chameleon
Ever warm, like a doting cat;

This macabre melody
Primed by the pen people
Pulling the wide world along
One smoldering bout of itchy fever.

---

* A god in Ayakoromo town, Delta State, Nigeria.

Plugging the holes

They always hold meetings
In the smug blackness of night
To tackle matters of state
As it were, plug the leaking sides
Of the proverbial ship.

How we give hot flesh
To the ancient myth
Of emptying one's fortune
When one sweeps out dirt
From the confines
Of a homely compound
After hens have come to roost–
The head a awry shadow.

O wedge the leaking sides
Of the heart's canoe
Fast sinking in the overcast skies
And howling waves and tides;
Who can mend the mangled moon
Far up the sockets of the sky
With haunting earthy voices
And covert steps of night men?

Who can pluck laughter
From a dumb giant
Gasping for breath
In a python's elastic mouth?
Potholes still everything
(Not only vehicular traffic)
On the sterile fields of men's heart
Despoiled from the garden of Eden
With multiple signatures against the spirit.

Let it be ingrained in the blood
Those who struggle to save their heads
Perish in their weak dream
Descanted even before cockcrow;
The woes of the weak
Enchant the unrepentant despot
Devoid of soul-searching song,

Like a dyed-in-the-wool lieutenant
Mining into brutish reservoirs
To daze a lily-chested acolyte
Whose fleeing boss fails to settle
A long overdue debt.

O these stilling potholes
The horrid handiwork
Of pathfinders with no soul;
Give a walking stick to a cripple
He lashes at you right away

Smothered by the strident colours
On your flag, hoisted
On far too high hills;
Smothered by your overbearing pastimes
The unbearable puff of your breath
Scattered on common souls
Without the echo of being
Eternal self-slaves; ensnared by hollow winds.

The laughter of light

The laughter of light is infinite
Swift in function
Like a hunter's hound
On the trail of fleeing antelopes
Or a coy cat catching a wakeful rat
Or a wall-gecko attacking
Some meddlesome insect.

No wonder brothers close their fields
Placing intruding light on permanent exile
At once a crown of the proverbial fleece
Turns stool-cloth, hosting
Some nebulous arses;

O the wizard of Amatebe*
The centre of his head
Laden with the lore of the land
Prowls stealthily with stunting powers
Locks away pens of sweating saplings
In a place beyond science or naked eyes.

And how they languish
In the heat waves of fruitless toil
Lashing at their souls
Hatchet men of night lords
Pelt their sleep and steps
With countless arcane arrows
Yanking open living graves.

A crowd of musketeers
Menacing in their bogus masks
Sullen in their nakedness
Walk the streets in sultry daylight
Blending with the light

Without seam or sweat-bath.

Nothing is utterly strange
Under the tropical sun
Debonairs in the day
Turn commanders at night.

Yet the bard's heart boils
Only school boys
Or kindergarten initiates
Sever infernal links
To open up
The Glory of all Lands ...

What happens to the fuming sires
In some nightly congregation
Or in dumb obeisance
To some dusky god
Mumbling some darksome thoughts
In the earlobes of some totem

Tucked well well away
In some nebulous corner
Covering quite some acres
And the shadow hanging in the horizon
Waxing stronger and stronger?

---

* A quarter in Bomadi, a riverine community in Delta State.

The dilemma of the passover train

Silent boos and jeers
Swamp the moralist on mere lips
Craving a smooth passage
To the ultimate light
Back-slapping soul mates
On buttered balconies;

And churlish charlatans
Wearing white smocks
Litter the terrace, harried
By their own hangovers.

Mired in the way of the age
They fill all interspaces–
A staircase to marble mountains
Where, like the crab, they pick
Their hearts' pearls with two hands.

It may linger a while
The captivity of white souls
Will linger a while ...

And their sanctified voices
Drowned in depths beyond
Ethereal divers of pearl;

And vendors of blood-sucking gods
Taunt the universe
With cloudy snapshots of the rainbow
Inscribed in the blood of martyrs
Yawning in their bums
Beyond the surface buntings
The painted revelry
The marble celebrations.

O this bard
Is in delirious anguish
Over the dilemma of the train:

Who do we pass over
With all souls lost to lust;
Even the finest fisher of men
Bathed a million times
In the baptism of the spirit
Oozes like rotten atabala* head

Or a fart saved for seven days
In a rumbling stomach?

---

*   Tilapia fish

A hollow claim

A sanctuary in a public square
Breeds squalid sires
Empty of the tiniest
Of the mind's ornaments

In secret scoffing laughter
At the propitious dream of the soul
Descending to the bowels of the earth.

Grandma says what is public
Is no longer a moral closet
Pulling together all kinds of pilgrims
Across the wide expanse of breath
A lot fanning the flesh–
The nebulous notion paradise ends
In pants, or in petals of purses;
Just a few the incandescent soul.

Take a stride of faith
Towards the fortress of the wise
Make oblation; seal a glowing fate
Just a step remains
And a fall on the stony path–
And the silence is eternal.

O what is sharpened in the spirit
Is set for war in the flesh
Not the hollow claims
Of brothers of the cross;

Without proper immersion in Pentecost
Clergymen ogle ravenously
At sumptuous handmaidens of the Lord
Setting the haunches even

Of a wrinkled old man on fire

Spreading like cancer
In the congregation–
To catch a manatee
Spread a big-eyed net
Across a shrub of elephant grass
On the seashore.

Remove the carapace of sanctimony
Swamping the altar
See hot beads of mating sweat
On the wrong mattress
In the cell along the passageway
To the inviolate sanctorium;

O remove the carapace of sanctimony
Swamping the altar
See globules of larceny
On disparate properties and purses.

The rats of McIver Waterside*

When the bait
Of a pugnacious patriot
Catches a big fish
His jaw bones drop
In disparate dumb gestures
In unorthodox paranoia
The eyes no longer see
Corpulent felons, ears deaf
To tales of fumbling fortresses

Pandering to shadowy controls
On the strings of the purse
And some poisoned bowls of honey–
A grumpy guillotine
Operated by some silent voices
In the sultry background
Bungling the pubescent rainbow
On the distant sky.

O no rat overfed
At McIver Waterside
Can jump over a barricade
Of seamless barbed wire
Even of the smallest height–
Meat for the roving cat;

No one faces a flare with fanfare
How can one quench Jesse fire
With mere spittle?
Even a phantom fan
Swells the flames, multiplying
The howling smoke in the horizon

Distil the protective mask
Over pongy winds
To sail to the pearls of the heart
Heightening the salty swing.

The stranger sinks in the waves
Oblivious of the gathering blood
In seascape memories
Oblivious of that impregnable Bomadi* myth
Of aborigines in a passover covenant
With the god of the beach.

This god, dripping with alien blood
Blind to the inviolate knot
Tying the brotherhood of man
Is in one long accord
With some occultic tree
In some aboriginal home
Along the creeks, stunted
Though untouched by man or storm

Offering ancestral cover
To assorted crooks
Who come from the clan
Through paternal or maternal routes
Who come in the cover of night
In secret supplication ...

The sore truth is
When the season
Fades into a graveyard
Night men enjoy a plumed passage
To the broad way, like
Those Abuja standard bearers
Saying a loud Aye to life pension
For bulging-stomached patriots
Who swallowed the rainbow in service

Preparing under-aged brides
To massage failing haunches at old age
Forgetting a sickle is not for
An unripe palm fruit
Forgetting the old man's farm diminishes.

And the tremors of the earth
Multiply, unending
Like cooking manatee meat
Leaving the last tongue of dissent
Floating in the hot afternoon wind
Of a yellow voyage into oblivion.

---

* In Warri, Delta State, Nigeria.
* A riverine community in Delta State, Nigeria.

Dreams

Ensconced in the yawning hole
Of a layabout's head
Are imperial strides
On the balcony of princes.

Hollow crevices
Are the mind's handmaiden
Coming from the unfathomable
Depths of the coast
Intangible yet concrete
Infinitesimal yet immense
Filling boundless voids
In their fleshy abstraction.

In the vast clearing
Of the mind
Lost stars find a way
To the main course
In dampening tunnels and turmoil;
Tendrils sprout beyond
Love's fertile furnace
Beyond Onobrakpeya's* animated colours

That beget swelling seasons
Stepping on star-lit staircases
To the howling wonders on mountaintops
In the ceaseless laughter of loins.

---

* Bruce Onobrakpeya– Nigerian printmaker, painter and sculptor.

Mystery

(for my mother's people)

I remember the forlorn footpath
To Kpakiama* market
Through the chilly
Precincts of Asiyaibou*
Exuding deep green vegetation
Unaxed and uncutlassed
From the beginning of things
Where birds sang enchanting tunes
In long deafening unison;
Here the ground was littered
With lush and lickable fruits
One couldn't pick, for fear
Of the god's wrath
Hanging on a still gust
Of wind, in the eerie horizon;
Was it not a strident taboo
To look left, where
The shrine was stationed,
So mortals did not
Behold a god's face?
O one thought
Man and god needed to tango
In one eternal clasp
Like mortar and pestle
To fashion a decent voyage
Against the roaring tide.

---

* Poet's maternal community in Delta State, Nigeria.
* A forest dedicated to a god.

Kraftgriots

Also in the series (POETRY) *continued*

Joe Ushie: *A Reign of Locusts* (2004)
Paulina Mabayoje: *The Colours of Sunset* (2004)
Segun Adekoya: *Guinea Bites and Sahel Blues* (2004)
Ebi Yeibo: *Maiden Lines* (2004)
Barine Ngaage: *Rhythms of Crisis* (2004)
Funso Aiyejina: *I,The Supreme & Other Poems* (2004)
'Lere Oladitan: *Boolekaja: Lagos Poems 1* (2005)
Seyi Adigun: *Bard on the Shore* (2005)
Famous Dakolo: *A Letter to Flora* (2005)
Olawale Durojaiye: *An African Night* (2005)
G. 'Ebinyo Ogbowei: *let the honey run & other poems* (2005)
Joe Ushie: *Popular Stand & Other Poems* (2005)
Gbemisola Adeoti: *Naked Soles* (2005)
Aj. Dagga Tolar: *This Country is not a Poem* (2005)
Tunde Adeniran: *Labyrinthine Ways* (2006)
Sophia Obi: *Tears in a Basket* (2006)
Tonyo Biriabebe: *Undercurrents* (2006)
Ademola O. Dasylva: *Songs of Odamolugbe* (2006), winner, 2006 ANA/Cadbury
     poetry prize
George Ehusani: *Flames of Truth* (2006)
Abubakar Gimba: *This Land of Ours* (2006)
G. 'Ebinyo Ogbowei: *the heedless ballot box* (2006)
Hyginus Ekwuazi: *Love Apart* (2006), winner, 2007 ANA/NDDC Gabriel Okara
     poetry prize and winner, 2007 ANA/Cadbury poetry prize
Abubakar Gimba: *Inner Rumblings* (2006)
Albert Otto: *Letters from the Earth* (2007)
Aj. Dagga Tolar: *Darkwaters Drunkard* (2007)
Idris Okpanachi: *The Eaters of the Living* (2007), winner, 2008 ANA/Cadbury
     poetry prize
Tubal-Cain: *Mystery in Our Stream* (2007), winner, 2006 ANA/NDDC Gabriel
     Okara poetry prize
John Iwuh: *Ashes & Daydreams* (2007)
Sola Owonibi: *Chants to the Ancestors* (2007)
Adewale Aderinale: *The Authentic* (2007)
Ebi Yeibo: *The Forbidden Tongue* (2007)
Doutimi Kpakiama: *Salute to our Mangrove Giants* (2008)
Halima M. Usman: *Spellbound* (2008)
Hyginus Ekwuazi: *Dawn Into Moonlight: All Around Me Dawning* (2008), winner,
     2008 ANA/NDDC Gabriel Okara poetry prize
Ismail Bala Garba & Abdullahi Ismaila (eds.): *Pyramids: An Anthology of Poems
     from Northern Nigeria* (2008)
Denja Abdullahi: *Abuja Nunyi (This is Abuja)* (2008)
Japhet Adeneye: *Poems for Teenagers* (2008)
Seyi Hodonu: *A Tale of Two in Time (Letters to Susan)* (2008)

120

Ibukun Babarinde: *Running Splash of Rust and Gold* (2008)
Chris Ngozi Nkoro: *Trails of a Distance* (2008)
Tunde Adeniran: *Beyond Finalities* (2008)
Abba Abdulkareem: *A Bard's Balderdash* (2008)
Ifeanyi D. Ogbonnaya: *... And Pigs Shall Become House Cleaners* (2008)
Ebinyo Ogbowei: *the town crier's song* (2009)
Ebinyo Ogbowei: *song of a dying river* (2009)
Sophia Obi-Apoko: *Floating Snags* (2009)
Akachi Adimora-Ezeigbo: *Heart Songs* (2009), winner, 2009 ANA/Cadbury poetry
    prize
Hyginus Ekwuazi: *The Monkey's Eyes* (2009)
Seyi Adigun: *Prayer for the Mwalimu* (2009)
Faith A. Brown: *Endless Season* (2009)
B.M. Dzukogi: *Midnight Lamp* (2009)
B.M. Dzukogi: *These Last Tears* (2009)
Chimezie Ezechukwu: *The Nightingale* (2009)
Ummi Kaltume Abdullahi: *Tiny Fingers* (2009)
Ismaila Bala & Ahmed Maiwada (eds.): *Fireflies: An Anthology of New Nigerian
    Poetry* (2009)
Eugenia Abu: *Don't Look at Me Like That* (2009)
Data Osa Don-Pedro: *You Are Gold and Other Poems* (2009)
Sam Omatseye: *Mandela's Bones and Other Poems* (2009)
Sam Omatseye: *Dear Baby Ramatu* (2009)
C.O. Iyimoga: *Fragments in the Air* (2010)
Bose Ayeni-Tsevende: *Streams* (2010)
Seyi Hodonu: *Songs from My Mother's Heart (2010),* winner ANA/NDDC Gabriel
    Okara poetry prize, 2010
Akachi Adimora-Ezeigbo: *Waiting for Dawn* (2010)
Hyginus Ekwuazi: *That Other Country* (2010), winner, ANA/Cadbury poetry prize,
    2010
Emmanuel Frank-Opigo: *Masks and Facades* (2010)
Tosin Otitoju: *Comrade* (2010)
Arnold Udoka: *Poems Across Borders* (2010)
Arnold Udoka: *The Gods Are So Silent & Other Poems* (2010)
Abubakar Othman: *The Passions of Cupid* (2010)
Okinba Launko: *Dream-Seeker on Divining Chain* (2010)
'kufre ekanem: *the ant eaters* (2010)
McNezer Fasehun: *Ever Had a Dear Sister* (2010)
Baba S. Umar: *A Portrait of My People* (2010)
Gimba Kakanda: *Safari Pants* (2010)
Sam Omatseye: *Lion Wind & Other Poems* (2011)
Ify Omalicha: *Now that Dreams are Born* (2011)
Karo Okokoh: *Souls of a Troubadour* (2011)
Ada Onyebuenyi, Chris Ngozi Nkoro, Ebere Chukwu (eds): *Uto Nka: An Anthology
    of Literature for Fresh Voices* (2011)
Mabel Osakwe: *Desert Songs of Bloom* (2011)
Pious Okoro: *Vultures of Fortune & Other Poems* (2011)
Godwin Yina: *Clouds of Sorrows* (2011)

Nnimmo Bassey: *I Will Not Dance to Your Beat* (2011)
Denja Abdullahi: *A Thousand Years of Thirst* (2011)
Enoch Ojotisa: *Commoner's Speech* (2011)
Rowland Timi Kpakiama: *Bees and Beetles* (2011)
Niyi Osundare: *Random Blues* (2011)
Lawrence Ogbo Ugwuanyi: *Let Them Not Run* (2011)
Saddiq M. Dzukogi: *Canvas* (2011)
Arnold Udoka: *Running with My Rivers* (2011)
Olusanya Bamidele: *Erased Without a Trace* (2011)
Olufolake Jegede: *Treasure Pods* (2012)
Karo Okokoh: *Songs of a Griot* (2012), winner. ANA/NDDC Gabriel Okara
        poetry prize, 2012
Musa Idris Okpanachi: *From the Margins of Paradise* (2012)
John Martins Agba: *The Fiend and Other Poems* (2012)
Sunnie Ododo: *Broken Pitchers* (2012)
'Kunmi Adeoti: *Epileptic City* (2012)
Ibiwari Ikiriko: *Oily Tears of the Delta* (2012)
Bala Dalhatu: *Moonlights* (2012)
Karo Okokoh: *Manna for the Mind* (2012)
Chika O. Agbo: *The Fury of the Gods* (2012)
Emmanuel C. S. Ojukwu: *Beneath the Sagging Roof* (2012)
Amirikpa Oyigbenu: *Cascades and Flakes* (2012)
Ebi Yeibo: *Shadows of the Setting Sun* (2012)
Chikaoha Agoha: *Shreds of Thunder* (2012)
Mark Okorie: *Terror Verses* (2012)
Clemmy Igwebike-Ossi: *Daisies in the Desert* (2012)
Idris Amali: *Back Again (At the Foothills of Greed)* (2012)
A.N. Akwanya: *Visitant on Tiptoe* (2012)
Akachi Adimora-Ezeigbo: *Dancing Masks* (2013)
Chinazo-Bertrand Okeomah: *Furnace of Passion* (2013)
g'ebinyŏ ogbowei: *marsh boy and other poems* (2013)
Ifeoma Chinwuba: *African Romance* (2013)
Remi Raji: *Sea of my Mind* (2013)
Francis Odinya: *Never Cry Again in Babylon* (2013)
Immanuel Unekwuojo Ogu: *Musings of a Pilgrim* (2013)
Khabyr Fasasi: *Tongues of Warning* (2013)
Immanuel Unekwuojo Ogu: *Musings of a Pilgrim* (2013)
Khabyr Fasasi: *Tongues of Warning* (2013)
J.C.P. Christopher: *Salient Whispers* (2014)
Paul T. Liam: *Saint Sha'Ade and Other Poems* (2014)
Joy Nwiyi: *Burning Bottom* (2014)
R. Adebayo Lawal: *Melodreams* (2014)
R. Adebayo Lawal: *Music of the Muezzin* (2014)

Printed in the United States
By Bookmasters